HANDWRITTEN BOOKS BY HENRY MILLER
1937–1940

The Book of Conversations with David Edgar
Given to David Edgar. Begun March 17, 1937.
Additional entries March 20, 25, April 10, 11, 15,
27, and May 2, 1937. Forthcoming from Sublunary
Editions (2023).

Order and Chaos Chez Hans Reichel
Given to Hans Reichel. Begun December 24, 1937.
Additional entries January 9, 13, 21, 25, 26, 28,
February 2 and 4, 1938. Published by Loujon Press
(1966).

Jupiter in All His Phases
Given to Lawrence Durrell. Begun April 20, 1938.
Additional entries April 21, July 22, September 25,
October 1, 5, 16, December 20 and 29, 1938; January
24, February 14, March 4, 10, 12, and 14, 1939.
Published by William Ashley (2022).

The Heaven Beyond Heaven
Given to Anaïs Nin. Begun early 1939. Additional
entries September 9, 14, December 11 and 21, 1939;
and January 12, 1940. Published by William Ashley
(2022).

The Waters Reglitterized
Given to Emil Schnellock. Begun February 22, 1939.
Additional entry March 12, 1939. Published by John
Kidis (1950), Capra Press (1973), and Village Press
(1973). Included in *Sextet*, published by Capra Press
(1977), Borgo Press (1978), John Calder (1980), and
New Directions (2010).

First Impressions of Greece
Given to George Seferis. Begun November 5, 1939.
Published by Capra Press (1973) and Village Press
(1973). Included in *Sextet*.

HENRY MILLER

JUPITER IN ALL HIS PHASES

Published by William Ashley

The manuscript of *Jupiter in All His Phases* has a running dialog on the recto pages with the verso pages having quotes, sayings and advice for Durrell. The paperback edition distributes the quotes to fill the blank verso pages as they are not linked to the running dialog. The Kindle version follows the order of pages in the manuscript, inserting the quotes, sayings and advice for Durrell indented in the dialog that had been opposite it. Some spelling has been changed to American rather than the British as Miller often used. Underlined words in the manuscript are italicized.

This book was written by Henry Miller in 1938 and 1939 and is previously unpublished.
Copyright © Estate of Henry Miller 2022.
First edition published by William Ashley, this printing with corrections on 1-26-2023
Library of Congress Cataloging-in-Publication-Data has been applied for
paperback: ISBN: 979-8-9860812-3-6
kindle: ISBN: 979-8-9860812-4-3
Printed by Epub on demand and available on Kindle
Available at Amazon.com

Lawrence Durrell was born at 1:00 am on February 27, 1912 in Jalandhar India. Jupiter is his dominant planet in a Sagittarian 1st house. He knew of Jupiter's influence on him from an early age. Conrad Moricand's horoscope, that Miller commissioned of Durrell, amplified what Miller felt about him. Durrell cherished that reading. He later wrote: "Rising Jupiter means luck in Springtime says the horoscope which the great astrologer Moricand once cast for me in Paris." [Notes on Travel by Durrell]

What Moricand saw was a complex man, capable of deception and intrigue, but good-natured—blessed with good fortune, sympathetic and attractive. As a Piscean, he saw him as subject to extremes—one who searches for the ideal. Jupiter endows him with good fortune and also makes him a creature of metamorphosis, a Proteus, who penetrates all things—a man of great style, intellectual, deeply intuitive—with great critical and analytical powers. He draws people to him with words. [The Big Supposer by Durrell]

Moricand's themes are repeated in the text of *Jupiter in All His Phases* with much advice for "Larry me Lad." There are quotes and insight into Miller's metaphysical journey. Henry wanted to attain satori, passing through the mouth of Draco into the Heaven Beyond Heaven as Lao-tse had done. There is insight into Miller's appreciation of Zen, the Occult, Astrology and Mysticism. He quotes from works by D. T. Suzuki, Éliphas Lévi, and Max Heindel. He notes the impact of Balzac's *Séraphîta* and *Louis Lambert*. Worried about the upcoming war, he believes astrology shows that Hitler will not prevail. He is looking forward to the age of Aquarius. Miller thought his horoscope predicted that he would achieve enlightenment on the spring equinox in 1942. He was going to tell his journey in *Draco and the Ecliptic*. When that did not happen, he felt that purging all his angst in the Rosy Crucifixion books would get him there.

As in the other five handwritten books that Miller wrote for his friends, his thoughts flow. There is little editing, great insights.... Wm. A.

Dummy Volume

Ref. No. *J.8257* Size *90 x 40*

Weight *80* Sheets *076*

Pages *900* Bulk *5/8 bore*

Quality *Not Antique Wo*

Cooking

LION   BRAND

JOHN DICKINSON & CO. LTD.
CROXLEY MILLS, WATFORD, HERTS
Mills Sales Office: 65 OLD BAILEY, LONDON, E.C.4

HENRY MILLER
18, Villa Seurat
PARIS (XIV)

"Jupiter in all his
phases."—Title.
By
Henry Miller
especially conceived
for his most Jup-
iterian friend—
Lawrence Durrell
of Burma, Nepal,
Tibet,   Paris,
Greece and all
holy places.
                1938.

For plasma I give you
magma, for doubt anguish,
for despair desperation,
for ecstasy exultation,
for mystery mysterium,
and for wistfulness the
eternal widdershins!
Faithfully yours,
my good sir—
Henry Valentine,
or just
HVM.
or
simply
"Val"

"Who dies not
before he dies,
is ruined when
he dies."
Jacob Boehme.
Author of that most
mystifying piece
of drollery—
"The Signature
of all Things."

_____

MYSTERY

"Draco": the 13th house of
the zodiac — into
which everything is refunded.
The hole in the top of
the universe — the heaven beyond
heaven.

 URANUS

JUPITER

 NEPTUNE

MYSTERY

"Draco": the 13th house of
the Zodiac—into
which everything is refunded.
The hole in the top of
the universe—the heaven beyond
heaven!

♅ URANUS

♃ JUPITER

♆ NEPTUNE

Zen has no "mind" to murder; therefore there is no "mind—murdering" in Zen. Zen has no "self" as something to which we can cling as a refuge; therefore, in Zen again there is no "self" by which we may become intoxicated.[1]

"The way to ascend unto God is to descend into one's self."[2]
Victor Hugo.

Unless we can break through the antithesis of "yes" and "no" we can never hope to live a real life of freedom.[3] (Zen)

To be free, life must be an absolute affirmation.[4] (Zen)

Any answer is satisfactory if it flows out of one's inmost being, for such is always an absolute affirmation.[5] (Zen)

The Zen master endeavors to take away all footholds which the disciple has ever had since his first appearance on earth and then to supply him with one that is really no foothold.[6]

I have been waiting for the right moment to begin the Jupiterian theme. Moricand, the astrologer, has been here all evening—left an hour ago. I have just had a walk around the Parc de Montsouris, past 21 Rue Gazan, eaten a bit of cheese and drank a tumbler of Châteauneuf du Pape.

Everything hinges on the color yellow, which as I was explaining to Moricand, I *discovered* some three or four years ago. Yellow is my color. It has to do with the attainment of wisdom. And wisdom has to do with the resolution of the conflict between matter and spirit. It is the symbolic color of the dragon which comes into its own when equilibrium is established and one acquires mastery of himself.

And where does Jupiter come in? I want to tell you about Jupiter from my intuitive understanding, not from what I have heard or read. I want first of all to abolish the notion of "luck" which seems to be attached to the name. Or rather, perhaps, I want to explain the deeper meaning of what is called "luck," chance, fortune, etc. How it is anything but hazardous. How it is something *realized*, if not earned.

Very oddly, I think immediately of Beethoven. I think of him as a man over whom Jupiter must surely have reigned. In him all the fatalities were utilized to the fullest measure. He went on from one misfortune to another, as if they were stepping stones to God. When I play the last quartet, which is brief, concise, quintessential—gay in "the happy rock" manner—I have a feeling that it represents the culmination of all that might be called Jupiterian. It seems to me that he expresses here at the very end the sense of liberation, amplitude and certainty. It is almost an algebraic expression in musical terms of the cosmic sense. If it has a mystic quality it reveals itself in its positiveness. Beethoven is at last the great whale with an ocean at his command.

Zen never explains (e'coute, Edgar!) but only affirms. Life is fact and no explanation is necessary or pertinent. To explain is to apologize *and why should we apologize for living*? To live— is that not enough?[7] *oui*! *oui*!

Zen abhors media, even the intellectual medium; it is primarily and ultimately a discipline and an experience, which is dependent on no explanation; for an explanation wastes time and energy and is never to the point; all that you get out of it is a misunderstanding and a twisted view of the thing.[8]

———————————

Divine or die! that was the ancient command.[9] Alors—die Rudolf and may you lie twisted forever in your iron logic!

He has found the source and revels in his discovery—or rather, his realization. The will has been drained dry; the male has reverted to the great fecundating female and found a new dimension in which to swim. It is a swimming now, and not a fight, a struggle. It is not a mellow music either, but a *yellow* music. Mellow is a word for maturity, but this which Beethoven asserts is beyond maturity—it is ageless. It belongs to no particular epoch; it is so thoroughly Beethoven that it has become universal, an accepted thing like the atmosphere, and so beyond praise or criticism.

Everybody speaks of the terrible misfortunes he endured and of how, finally, he learned to accept the blows and to use them for his own inner development. But this, it seems to me, is the very crux of the Jupiterian theme: the dual aspect of what is called fortune or misfortune. In other words, the understanding of the word "destiny," and of emancipation through necessity. Through touching despair, through wallowing in desperation.

If, when Edgar speaks of a Jupiter "badly aspected," he means the failure "to realize" the nature of one's destiny, then I agree with him. But it seems to me also that no one who is really an artist, as you are, can escape this knowledge. It is the classic thing—the Oedipean line, as it were—to try to escape one's destiny. But we who know the tragedy of Oedipus are hardly likely to repeat the myth. The human race repeats it because it is the destiny of the race to become individualized—and perhaps pass on into another type of living creature. The artist is only making the race aware of its limitations, of its necessity to surpass itself. The creative instinct I see as bound up in the sense of the fatal, which is neither good nor bad, neither fortune or misfortune. This cosmic sense is simply the affirmation of the continuous process of life in all its paradoxical manifestations. Jupiter has all the resonance of this paradoxical knot which we must undo by living.

11

"Your every-day life—that is the Tao!"[10]

In other words, a quiet, self-confident, truthful existence of your own—that is the truth of Zen.[11]

Listen, Larry me lad—at the very top of the vault there is a great hole and this hole is the famous dragon of the apocalypse—*Draco*, as he was known to the Babylonians. It is the constellation which makes the *13th* house of the zodiac. When Lao-tse went over the mountains he passed into Draco, the heaven beyond heaven.

Q. What are you doing here?
A. I am not doing anything.
R. If so you are idling your time away.

Is not idling the time away doing something?[12]
   Oi'll say so!!

(Gracie)

And now it is three months later and I am sitting in the American Hospital at Neuilly waiting for the doctor to arrive—he is cutting up lungs at present, it seems. I have just explained to my translator, who is obliged to write a preface to the French edition of "Tropic," that I promise the world for the year 1942 a "mystical" work, to be called "Draco and the Ecliptic"—because in 1942 I shall be passing my own ecliptic and will have emerged into the "heaven beyond heaven." This means that the Shangri-la which one creates and escapes to during the time of stress must give way to an acceptance of the world in which whatever was acquired through the womb life in the Himalayas of the soul must be restored to man in person. The account must be settled, in other words. The individual must return to the stream of life, not only biologically, but spiritually. Even the spiritual heritage must be sacrificed, abandoned, on entering the heaven beyond heaven. "God giveth and God taketh away," say the scriptures—but God too must be nourished. For the world to be truly alive and to sing in all its parts what is God in man must be delivered up to the world. God must be consumed and subsumed.

"When you realize that the mind is no mind, you understand the mind and its workings."[13] (Zen)

"When a thing has its fixed abode it is fettered, it is no more absolute."[14] (Zen)

Little did I dream, when I wrote the last page at the American Hospital that the next one would be from Bordeaux! Edgar went to London with a trunkful of mystical books—to study occultism at first hand. Fred was last seen hovering around his domicile at the Impasse Rouèt. Reichel grew a mustache during his stay at the psychopathic ward. And so on.

Ever since you left I have been seeing Moricand regularly, and learned a tremendous lot from him. I learned also something about Paracelsus, Hermes Trismegistus and "*Séraphîta*," by Balzac, perhaps one of the strangest books ever written.

I finished *Capricorn* by sheer grit and will, driven on by some deep presentiment of the break-up impending. In fact, during my four years—exactly four years!—at the Villa Seurat, I accomplished most everything I set out to accomplish. I have had to leave behind a lot of things I regard as rather precious, but I have a blind faith that they will not be destroyed—that no matter how great the destruction and confusion some one will some day rescue them and bring them to light. Just last Sunday, a week ago, and still no thought of leaving, Moricand read off to Fred and me a list of the great libraries of the past and of what was supposed to have been lost with their destruction. An amazing number of books—and a still more amazing list of their contents. And yet, when he read it off to us, I felt that nothing was really lost. What man truly acquires sticks—that's my belief. But what is really assimilated by man is pathetically little. It is a snail's pace. I see the human race very much like the orbital movements of the planets—some very close and spinning faster and faster—others way out at the rim and hardly seeming to move at all, hardly even

turning on their own axis. And every once in a while, almost as if God had to do a cosmological piece of calculus, there is a world-wide reckoning, an addition or subtraction, in which the individual seems to be completely ignored and only a profit and loss for the human race is noted.

However bad things may be these coming days— or months or years—it is not the end, as some imagine. Certain problems which agitate us now will drop entirely out of consciousness. It's a crude way of solving things—but it's the cosmological way. It's also a sort of instinctive way to rise above (or sink below) the opposites.

For me to be in Bordeaux is something almost unimaginable. What am I doing here? How did I happen to be here? It's a mystery—one of those accidents which happens when the cards are shuffled for a new deal. I did my part at the Villa Seurat. I've done all it was humanly possible to do. Now I am marking time, and letting God take a hand and run the show as it suits him. I am almost in a trance. I do nothing all day but walk about the town, looking at shoes, hats, corsets, umbrellas, pharmaceutical supplies and so on. I read nothing but the newspapers—each fresh bulletin. I seem to have predicted all this—and still it's always a surprise. You never expect to be in Bordeaux, or whatever it may be, but always in some more familiar place. The strange thing is, that for quite some time I have wanted to go to Toulouse. In fact, when I left Paris, I thought I was heading in that direction. I always imagine that some wonderful experience lies in wait for me at Toulouse. (But everybody says don't go—it's uninteresting.) Perhaps I will still be writing you from there. We'll see.

Anyway here I am in Bordeaux—or the part of me that eats and drinks and looks vacantly into shop-windows. The planet Jupiter is still shining bright in the sky. It has been gleaming like a million carat diamond for the last two months.

19

———————————————

*** "When the mind is ready for some reasons or others, a bird flies, or a bell rings, *and you at once return to your original home*, this is, you discover your now real self."[15] (Zen) ***

———————————————

———————————————

———————————————

According to the astrologers it is the present "opposition" between Jupiter and Mars which is causing all the trouble. I might interpret that broadly by saying that it represents a conflict between the cosmic sense of things, the essential wisdom of things, and the will. Jupiter is hanging in the Western sky—Mars in the East. The dividing line is really the frontier between Germany and France.

At this point interrupted by the startling news—one ultimatum after another. It is over now—an "accord" has been reached. But it marks the end of another epoch in our history.

Lourdes (Pyrenees)	*October 1st*
	New Calendar Commences

Decided to come here for a bit of peace after the depressing events of the last few weeks. The city of miracles! I get off the train in a downpour and start down the main drive in search of a cheap hotel. Almost immediately I fall into a street which is full of shops where they sell souvenirs. The whole damned street, I tell you, from one end to the other, and not a customer in sight. This is the ghostliest sight imaginable—especially at such a moment. Here they are, the human lice, selling post-cards of the miracle, and shoe horns and canes and pin cushions and ash-trays. God, what a sight! I get the horrors. An hour after I've taken a room I tell the patrone that I'm going to leave for Toulouse. She asks me have I seen the "grotto" yet. No, I haven't. I'm letting her persuade me to stick it out another day.

I'll go to see the discarded crutches at the church. I'll take a motor car and see the "Cirque Gavarnie." Then out and away—to the cities! Nature drives me crazy. Small towns and small people drive me crazy. I don't want to travel. I want merely to see something really different—something *grand*. Coming down that street with the souvenirs, I got to laughing hysterically. Had to hold my hand over my mouth. It's the first time I've laughed in weeks—or even smiled. Here it's as though nothing happened. They won't feel the repercussion for years to come. But we of the big cities know what has happened. The death begins at the tips of the branches. They think, poor devils, that they have made peace. They've signed Europe's death warrant, that's what it amounts to. I tell you, we will be driven to go to Tibet. The order of man which we represent has no counterpart here any more. He's surrendered. I can see myself traveling like this from place to place and things getting blacker and blacker. I want to see the men of the new order—of the coming "root race." This cycle is finished. War or peace—it makes no difference. It's the end.

Well, we got the *Black Book* out anyway—that's something. And I'll keep after Kahane to bring out *Capricorn*. There may be no more volumes but this one. Because there will be no readers. We will have to learn a new language, a code language, for those to come after us. It's terrible to be right and to see your predictions fulfilled, in your own lifetime. Events are moving faster than we can prophesy.

Pluto, the last planet to be discovered, is the sign of death and resurrection. It is the double-faced planet. The Germans will take care that we get the "death." It is up to us to usher in the "resurrection." Larry, me lad, gird up your loins. The world awaits you!

The most harrowing recollection I have of the crisis—the death, you might say—

For Edgar to note—"However deep one's knowledge of abstruse philosophy, it is like a piece of hair flying in the vastness of space!"[16] (Zen)

(note: It was this invisible, indestructible hair that St. Francis held on to. He should have let it go, Chesterton to the contrary. Much as I admire him, I prefer Nijinsky or even poor Louis Lambert.)

is the picture of the old buzzards in the cafés at Bordeaux. The day after peace was declared, when by all that is human and holy, people should have been dancing and weeping and falling into each other's arms, there were these buggers playing cards just as before. That infuriated me more than anything. What's to be done with the card-players? What good peace if this thing is to continue indefinitely? And the young healthy ones went off to the front without a word of protest. That too was a horrible sight. I'll never forget it. This time the war hit home. For a whole month that bugger Hitler dangled it before our eyes. What a Cagliostro! No wonder he doesn't have to fire a gun—he gives a local anesthetic and calmly proceeds to amputate another limb. He leaves the head for the last. That will make a nice dish of brains—an hors d'oeuvre for the warriors when the day is won and they sit down to the final feast.

Marseilles–*Oct.* 5th

After Lourdes comes Toulouse, even worse from the point of view of architecture. A city so consistently ugly, neutral, monotonous, that I thought I had been shunted back in my sleep to Brooklyn. I take a room in the biggest hotel—The Grand Hotel. It's like a Turkish bath emporium. This city is fifty years behind every other city in France. The people are tremendously alive and animated but thoroughly uninteresting, the remnant of some degenerate stock, probably Catalan, which one encounters all through the midi. I find the south everywhere—in every country—sad, depressing. The gayety is forced—it's only to keep them from committing suicide. They have nothing to do, and no desire to do anything. Life has passed them by—they are living in a backwash. It is a great error to call these people gay. One has to be a colossus to support the emptiness of this life of the South. What makes it more hideous to me is

that the life flow was arrested before they had reached the point of decadence. I don't mind at all being among super-civilized, worn-out decadent peoples. In fact I prefer it. What I can't stand are peasants, degenerate descendants of older races in whom there is not a spark of the past.

I stayed overnight in Toulouse, and then took the train to Nimes where there is a great Roman amphitheater and where ten years ago I saw my first bull-fight. This time I couldn't stand the place. Engaged rooms in three different hotels, walked around for an hour or so, took a drink and decided to flee. Only five in the afternoon and the sun already dead—that quick twilight, cold, gloomy, austere, which you get in the southern climes. I hate it! I prefer the honest gloom of the north, which begins at noon, or even in the morning. I don't like a brief spell of sunshine and everybody sitting around and pretending that it is really not winter. The South is a twilight world! One can freeze to death in these "warm" places.

Anyway, I don't want to see any more of Europe, no matter how beautiful. I want to see an entirely different world, different races, different customs. I would like to see the Javanese or the Balinese. Not Tahiti, that's already choked with Pernod and syphilis. Something older, super-civilized, decadent to the nth degree. I have no interest in Europe's half-baked culture. And I am afraid that the Chinese have taken the wrong path, that after this war they will become still more Europeanized, and rapidly. They have chosen Progress instead of Reality. Where to go? And how? I can see myself returning to the Villa Seurat and sitting there in an opium trance with arms folded and eyes half-closed.

The new world is not evident yet anywhere—only in the hearts of a few people. I feel I am being obliged to lead a nomadic existence again—not in search of a "place" but in search of a few rare comrades.

"*Satori* comes upon a man unawares, when he feels that he has exhausted his whole being."[17] (Zen)

"*Satori* is the *raison* d'être of Zen without which Zen is no Zen."[18] (This is a master-piece of Japanese syllogistic phlogiston of epistemological pseudomorphosis.)

I feel certain that only a larger conception of life can stay the impending debacle. Everything we have participated in will go. I can see a great eruption taking place, followed by a long night of anarchy in which the ground will be prepared for an utterly new way of life, one in which all these petty problems of politics, armaments, food and shelter will no longer exist. The men of five hundred years hence will marvel at the banality of our problems. For intelligent sensitive people these problems are null.

However, this explains it:—"In Zen *there must be Satori*; there must be a general mental upheaval which destroys the old accumulations of intellection and lays down the foundation for a new life."[19]

(Edgar is on the brink of discovering or experiencing *satori*. Satori, I might say, speaking professionally is the germinal reside of what in the west is called neurosis, but which is really the *Devil in mental guise*. Satori returns him to the void where evil rules without let or hindrance.)

To my astonishment everybody has resumed his tasks, his old way of life. I can't get over it. For me it *was* a war and a death. Never in the history of the world has such a miracle occurred as the last minute truce. Yet nobody seems fundamentally changed except myself. The gulf between myself and the rest of mankind has widened to a terrifying degree. I have never known such loneliness, such despair. Wherever I go, I see death. It is exactly as though I were living in hell—it is more real even than any hell I could imagine.

Today I was reading an essay on marine life—on the metabolism of deep sea fish. Suddenly, as I was reading it, it occurred to me that for the greater part of humanity the whole existence is passed deep below the surface. A life in the dark passed in killing and plundering. And even if they wished to come to the surface and see the world as it is it would be disastrous—it would mean death too. What seems like a law is that life must go on on different levels, that each level or stratum must live out its cycle, its destiny.

The fatality of the present conflict (which may continue for a century or two, for all we know) seems so clear that it paralyzes me. Putting words together seems like a capitulation to false hope. I see no hope for the great body of men. Their faces are like barometers to me. There is no light shining in their eyes—nothing which promises to raise them above the conflict, which is the only escape from doom. These are the faces of the lost and damned. And I myself feel lost and damned so long as I remain among them. At the very moment when I thought I had solved my personal problems, when I had found a way of life which suited me, when I had raised myself above this stupid drama in which the world is engulfed,

31

Le Musicien
d'autrefois!
HM.

"No one is isolated in this world; each is a fatality or a providence."[20] Éliphas Lévi

———————————————

(a marvelous thought! The only isolation is the pseudo-isolation achieved by the neurotic. That is why it is "a *living* death." Only God can become truly dead—but he has no desire to. Man *knows* death by refusing to become God.)

I find myself threatened more seriously than ever. One cannot make a haven on the edge of a volcano which is still emptying. One cannot persuade a volcano to become a still and quiet mountain. A philosophy of life which refuses to take cognizance of the existence of the volcano is stupid and futile. What makes it worse is that this volcano is *human* and embraces nearly the whole world.

More and more I come to believe that the great cataclysms of nature which accompany the end of great cycles of life are brought about by man himself. I believe that the way man lives determines the character and the orbit of the earth— and consequently even the pattern of the stars. I think we bring about the configurations in the sky as we bring about the configurations here below—and even below our feet! I believe that everything which makes up Reality is the result of our desires. It is just this fact that man holds it within his power to make life as he chooses which makes the fatality of this present situation so terrifying to me. It seems to me he has not the least desire to make it any different than it now is. The hell he has chosen is so marvelously adapted to his taste that the world is stuck tight in a glue. To move one way would mean the recovery of his instincts; to move the other way would set him on the spiritual path. He is so completely unfit for either that he can not be budged. He is caught in a vise of his own making and everything he suffers is more real than if he enjoyed freedom of one sort or another. It is the perfect picture of hell—the prisoner condemned to live in "the world of effects."

Only those who are already dead (who are sound asleep) are privileged to know such a condition. And *I* am not asleep and not dead. I am wide awake and boiling in horror. *I* know that the spell can be broken, and broken only by coming alive in the true sense. For man, it seems to me, has been dead from eternity! He has never opened his eyes, never lived—*as a human being.*

"The head of the horse's vital body (as was the case with Louis Lambert) is far outside the head of its dense body. The two points are closer together in the dog than in any other animal *except, perhaps,* (sic!) the elephant. When they come into correspondence we have an animal prodigy, able to count, spell, etc."[21]

Max Heindel

Perhaps this is the turning point, the awakening. Otherwise, I feel he will never again have the opportunity—he will relapse into some inert form of life, become in fact the fossil which he now seems. And I mean this very seriously. It is so real and so dramatic that it kills words. Everything that one *is* he must now exemplify to the fullest. In action or inaction—but not in words any longer. The wires have broken down. The symbols must communicate with one another directly.

"Had that regime (of the Lucifer Spirits) lasted *man would have remained simply a God-guided automaton* and would never have become a personality—an individual."[22]

Max Heindel

(As usual, Max is right—but at what a price, *individuality*! I should prefer to be—speaking solely for myself, of course, "a God-guided automaton.")

If I had a horse and buggy I would go for a buggy ride. If I had just a sleigh I would go for a sleigh ride. The femme de ménage has just left and the place smells sweetly of Eau de Javel, which is French for lysol. Eau de Javel not only cleans floors and sinks, but also prevents conception. It does not make for metamorphosis, however. For that Jupiter is necessary—and he is especially metamorphic (like gneiss rock) when found in his own house, which is Sagittarius. Jupiter, when he is not crippled or defective or afflicted, often gets drunk on his own sperm. Jupiter is the God of expansiveness—and therefore never found in the pantheon of French deities. His vice is giving, his weakness is a tendency to absorb too much. Whence the sclerotic maladies, such as penury, hemorrhoids and hidden fungi. Jupiter, to consolidate his god-like virtues, needs to be balanced like Libra or Virgo, the latter especially, since it is the house of the antiquary, the refuge of bright souls like Goethe and George Washington. Virgo is what makes you hold on to old shoes, old cravats, old suspenders— what makes it difficult, when you are breaking up house, to separate yourself from slightly used carbon paper, unfinished rolls of toilet paper, clips, blotters, pencil stubs and old love letters. Virgo is the sign of the British Museum, of the Louvre, of all undertaking establishments and of French finance in general. Virgo is never without a shirt to its name. Never! Whereas Jupiter is apt to give his wife's petticoats to the first-comer. Jupiter tips prodigally and repents secretly. Jupiter is also what saves the universe from the scourge of entropy. It gives without running down like a clock—because it always replenishes itself like a thief. The curse of Jupiter is that it gives what does not belong to it. For at bottom Jupiter is proud, possessive and secretive. Jupiter is regal like a god. But nature is blindly prodigal.

"So from discovery to discovery *we shall work back* to Hermetic philosophy, and shall be astonished at those prodigies of Simplicity and brilliance which have been for so long and long forgotten."[23]

Éliphas Lévi.

"Today is the time of Virgil the universe is in expectation"[24]

ditto

(Note: I am perhaps the only man in the world today who realizes that in *Séraphita* Balzac performed for the men of Aquarius what Virgil in his 4th Eclogue performed for the men of Pisces. A very great secret is embedded in this book—and I have discovered it!)

Jupiter always knows why and *to whom* to give—even when he seems to be reckless and blind.

Jupiter always knows on which side his bread is buttered. He suffers from subliminal consciousness. His secret drug is luminal [phenobarbital]. Luminal calms the hysteria and the epileptic, but it also lights the path of the awoken one. Fully awakened, Jupiter is invincible. But Jupiter's tragedy is to believe that the world revolves about himself. Jupiter is the genuine solipsist par excellence. Hence madness if bulked too long.

About his sperm again... How Jupiter is never promiscuous, despite all outward appearance. Jupiter merely loves to fecundate. Jupiter is happy shooting sperm into anything—ideas, cunts or cadavers. Jupiter doesn't give a fuck about fucking *per se*. Jupiter fucks to make people dance, to shake white rabbits out of black hats. Jupiter, in his right senses, would just as lief fuck a cellar door or a sewer grating. Thus he is often saddled not only with the venereal diseases, but with the scorbutic and bubonic plagues. He must be careful of garbage, fat rats and arsenic compounds.

Jupiter makes his best impression on miserly souls, on all those who have never opened up or refuse to open up. He is like a shower of manna to the poor at heart.

"Systems which are now in warfare are dreams of twilight: *let them pass.*"[25]
"Truth has no past and no future; it is eternal; *it is not that which ends; it is our dream only.*"[26]

Éliphas Lévi.

To which I say, with a great shout of joy— *d'accord*!
(Edgar to the contrary notwithstanding! The difference between us? *I have known evil*! Let him guard the doctrine. I claim the soul—*and the heart*!)

London, *Dec. 29th*

London, when all circumstances are favorably conjoined, is the beloved octopus of the world. Her centrality is in the tentacles, in the omnivorous and devouring clutch. She is the world-mother which renews creation by devouring her young. She also purveys high-class meat now and then, especially in the St. Pancras district where the pubs are crammed with male and female singers who are waiting for the depression to pass.

"Not even the highest evolved being on earth is capable of unveiling the Ego of the humblest and least developed creature. That, and that alone upon earth, is so sacred that it is absolutely safe from intrusion."[27]

Max Heindel

(This is the secret of my defeat at the hands of my wife June—the greatest lesson I had to learn!)

"Were the present rulers of the masses able to govern *themselves* we should again have the Millennium or Golden Age."[28]

Max Heindel

London was like a dose of cheer and kindliness—the world of harmlessness. Paris wakes one up again—with ideas, plans, projects, dreams, faces, new terrors, new anxieties. Paris is the soul of the world which is constantly being used up. Paris creates death through wakefulness. One has to leave Paris, like one leaves a too interesting book, in order to assimilate in peace and quiet the multiplicity of things which willy-nilly one ingests. Paris is the womb of the civilized world, with an ulcer eating it away. It tries to pretend that it has no connection with the vagina. That's why so much rape. Everything bubbles and seethes here. Very little gets properly expressed. The transmogrification has to be carried out elsewhere.

Feb. 14th –1:00 A.M.

If there is a new order coming it must be a Jupiterian one— the horn of plenty, for everyone. I'm beginning to get an image, a pre-vision of the coming world. I can see how the catastrophes are ushering in the good—bringing about a leaven. I see that the crude workings in groups, cults, nations, races, the war of ideologists everywhere, is only expressive of the hidden doctrines propagated by the "initiates." There is nothing to fear about the destruction ensuing, because the upheaving force is a life force—generative, regenerative. It's only the pressure of dead & crystallized forces which produce the explosions. The occultists say the earth tends "to soften," to become less rigid. A wonderful thought. Because the earth too is only a form, a condensed manifestation of the life within. Help loosen the crust, help soften the earth! Let the life stir more freely!

"Magical science is the absolute science of equilibrium."[29]

Éliphas Lévi

(But not in the French sense of the word!— HM.)

"Thus all dies because all lives, and if it were possible to make any form eternal, then motion would be arrested *and the only real death would be thus created.*"[30]

Éliphas Lévi

(Echoing my last Hamlet letter)

When you think of the way our lives are held in check, "in place," so to speak, you begin to realize how closely human life resembles earth-life, with mineral, stone, fossil, etc. All the forces of preservation—law, government, education, etc.—are the cramping, restrictive forces of death. I notice that the occultists ask—not how did life come to be?—for *that* they take for granted, as the cardinal unquestionable fact; but rather, "how did these dead things come to be? Why corpses? Why death?" Bravo, I say. The right way to put the query. Life is. Death is only a negation, a denial. From death life. It's life everywhere, and death is only a name supplied in ignorance and fear.

This idea not only stands things (or men) upside down, but inside out. I believe that death is like a meeting place of conflicting forces, whence it is no longer possible to turn inside out. One stops where one's vision ends. It's really not a point or place, but a focus. When one can no longer move the lens around. The moment we really begin to think about the world, our lives, ourselves, things change radically. Very very few people are thinking. What is called thinking is mere automatism—reflex action of the cerebro-spinal system. The skeleton is talking—not the blood.

All our systems would crumble over-night once we seriously began to think. By that, I mean *meditate*. The opposite of voluntary effort. The creation of the artist only begins at the moment of surrender. He can use his will to concentrate upon his theme, but the inspiration and the urge to do only comes when he has opened up, when he becomes fecundable. The male in him is only the spirit in search of reality. Reality is his goal—but reality is ever-present, on tap, so to speak. When he lays his egg, it is thru his female self, which has had the wisdom to be still and to brood and hatch. His grand ideas exist eternally—pre-existed and post-exist. He merely goes to the warehouse,

47

"The Lemurian had no eyes... While the
Sun was within—while the Earth formed
part of the light giving mass—man needed
no external illuminant; he was luminous
himself."31

(Max Heindel)

Bravo! J'y crois absolument. Heureusement,
comme dit la petite Anaïs dans son "Journal"—
"quand l'une s'eteint l'autre s'allume."

    Y'en a, même d'aujourd'hui, de nos jours,
qui gardent les deux lumières. Mais leurs noms
sont inconnus.

[Bravo! I absolutely believe it. Fortunately, as
little Anaïs says in her Journal—"when one goes
out the other lights up." There are some, even of
our time, nowadays, who keep the two lights on.
But their names are unknown.]

"Birth and death involved no break in the
consciousness and were therefore nonexistent
to the Lemurians. "32
              Max Heindel
(This is a gem, which I understand perfectly,
even if it should not be true.)

Then this idiocy....
"... but they did not make the Lemurian morbid,
because he had no memory."

(*NOTE*: All my sympathies are with the
Lemurian!)

if he is patient enough to wait and have the key brought to him. Everything is "on the ice," has been lying in cold storage for him since eternity. His whole life, as artist, is only a preparation for, or initiation into, a higher, larger life, wherein he will function anonymously. His creative torments are only birth-pangs on the way to ordination. As artist he is still an equation. As a full-fledged man he becomes a number. As number he is prophetic and visionary. He achieves "infinite egress," because freed from the obsessions of form. The world of forms is three- dimensional, demands tension, and suffers pain and sorrow. There are endless nirvanas, I fully believe. Each nirvana is merely the awareness of the preceding illusion of form or idea. A halting-place. A hatching-place for the soul. But the soul is an endless onion. The last layer will never be peeled. The conception of "last" dies out first. Every conception and perception dies out. If you can imagine an expanding consciousness with an ever-increasing faculty of remembrance, you can also imagine that these two factors must inevitably change so radically that as they approach the infinite of reality, they no longer resemble either memory or consciousness. It is like the Sun behind the Sun—the one we never see, but which we know of through seeing the glowing orb of the focused lens every day. But the white invisible Sun is not revealed to us, until, at least, we feel it in ourselves. I shudder with delight in anticipation of the great, the staggering discoveries yet to be made—above and below! We are just poking around on the thin outer membrane of hazardous speculation. Our great natural laws (sic!) are only the reflections of our poverty-stricken imagination. This holds good as well for "occult" science as for "material" science.

Whatever is to be discovered will only be evolved out of the inner vessel or vehicle. I tell you, the day will come when *all* the instruments will be thrown away—as well as the civil codes and the pieces of foolish money and

49

"*The Lucifer Spirits*! These spirits were a class of stragglers in the life wave of the Angels."[33]

(sic)

(The gibberish of profundity.)

———————————————

————————————

————————————

To be matched only by the dull idiocies of Rudolf Steiner and his horde of elemental aorists.

"Speech may be uttered in vain, but in itself it cannot be vain, and it has a meaning invariably. *Whatsoever has a name exists!*"[34]

Éliphas Lévi

"It may be understood in a day to come that seeing is actually speaking and that the consciousness of light is a twilight of eternal life in being."[35]

Éliphas Lévi

"All enthusiasms are comparative and graduated manias."[36]

ditto

"He who isolates himself is given over to death thereby..."[37]

ditto

(Pass this onto Fraenkel!)

all the other flub-dub. One can see infinitely more *without* the instruments. They are only crutches of the fettered imagination. The only science is the Law which is open to every one to read by merely closing his eyes. Everything is engraved in the heart. The heart will be more and more the supreme ruling organ. (Black-out until 5,000 A.D.)

If sometimes I seem to live too much in the future it is only because this is all so surely dead and finished that I can scarcely contain myself. I *know* what sort of life lies ahead of us. I can jump a few thousand years—with ease. I tell you it will not be at all a "scientific" age, in the sense now predicted. The scientific will have become rudimentary knowledge, absorbed by the vegetative system. There will be marvelous "free-wheeling"—take it from me. We are now climbing the mountain of awareness. We haven't yet had a glimpse of the valley on the other side.

But I know that a rich meadow land lies in wait. I can smell the clover and the alfalfa—and a bit o' sassafras too. There the rock-breaking "saxifrage" which Séraphîta plucked for Minna will be found in abundance. In the first spring of the 19th century it was miraculous to come upon it. Thats why Balzac was so elated. But, as he says of himself (for *he* was the dual Séraphitüs = Séraphîta), "I am blessed with vision." "My eyes give out light." Oh yes, and many more wonderful things. He saw the whole century clearly, and into the past and future both. He split on the vision. His whole gigantic creation—almost inhuman in its abundance—was nothing more than the splitting of the egg of knowledge. He opened up worlds in that pathogenetic split. It was the "grand écart" in the music-hall of eternity. No trapeze stunt with parasol and cane, á la Cocteau. But a spiritual hatching whose cuneiform legend he gave us in "*Séraphîta*" and "Louis Lambert."

New 'Verve' Issue Features
Material on Apocalypse

128 Pages of Reproductions and
Articles

The spring issue of "Verve," of which
the American number has just appeared, contains a lavish collection of
art and oddity.

Scattered through its 128 pages are
numerous reproductions in color, ranging from the work of eleventh-century
illuminators down through Giotto, Uccello, Bosch, Ingres and Renoir to the
latest paintings of Georges Braque and
original colored lithographs by Kandinsky and Masson. There is an abundance of photographs, and the textual
portion, much of which is illustrated
by curious old drawings and engravings, is by such writers as James Joyce,
Ernest Hemingway, André Gide, Paul
Valéry, André Malraux and Henri Michaux.

An outstanding feature of the new
number is the section devoted to the
Apocalypse, a theme which especially
appealed to the somber medieval imagination. Illuminations, strange in
conception and exotic in color, are reproduced from little-known eleventh,
thirteenth and fifteenth-century manuscripts, and are accompanied by a
violent essay on the Apocalypse by
André Suarès.

Another curiosity is an eight-page
section of colored lithographs reproducing a sort of series of esoteric puzzles
from a medieval work on astrology.

[clipping pasted in] **New 'Verve' Issue Features Material on Apocalypse 128 Pages of Reproductions and Articles** The spring issue of "Verve," of which the American number has just appeared, contains a lavish collection of art and oddity. Scattered through its 128 pages are numerous reproductions in color, ranging from the work of eleventh-century illuminators down through Giotto, Uccello, Bosch, Ingres and Renoir to the latest paintings of Georges Braque and original colored lithographs by Kandinsky and Masson. There is an abundance of photographs, and the textual portion, much of which is illustrated by curious old drawings and engravings, is by such writers as James Joyce, Ernest Hemingway, André Gide, Paul Valéry, André Malraux and Henri Michaux. An outstanding feature of the new number is the section devoted to the Apocalypse, a theme which especially appealed to the somber medieval imagination. Illuminations, strange in conception and exotic in color, are reproduced from little-known eleventh, thirteenth and fifteenth-century manuscripts, and are accompanied by a violent essay on the Apocalypse by André Suarès. Another curiosity is an eight-page section of colored lithographs reproducing a sort of series of esoteric puzzles from a medieval work on astrology.

52

March 4, 1939

How true the above was I did not realize until I picked up a book today on the Quai dealing with the prophecies of *Nostradamus*. The book ends on this note—the true meaning of Balzac's "*Séraphîta*." The coming, in other words, of the angel when man will really liberate himself from the thralldom of the animal world. *When?* After we have passed through the 2160 year cycle of the Aquarian Age into which we are now slipping, or have already slipped, into for possibly the last hundred years. In short, until we come back again to Aquarius—the course of a solar year: 25,960 years! But it will happen on a *new* continent to rise up out of the sea. I believe it absolutely. That continent will probably be in the region of the Americas—my guess is somewhere around the Isthmus of Panama and all the sunken region which makes the great deltoid basin of the Amazon.

Everything I read in the occult and prophetic books I seem to have already previsaged. It is all familiar to me, and soundly in accord with my own intuitions. All except the *language*. Moricand, in responding to a recent *enquête* by Volontés, gives a description of this new Soul & geologic cartography—asking at the end "who will be the Virgil that will give us the 4th Eclogue for the Aquarian Age?"[38]

Et bien, mon vieux, ou ça sera vous ou moi—ou tous les deux! Quand j'ai lu Hermès Trismégiste, j'ai reconnu mon vrai maître, qui n'était d'autre, sans doute, que moi-même dans une incarnation autreieme. Quand j ai lu Lao-tsé, c'était même plus frappant! J'ai reconnu mon propre sourire où il y avait de la magie, la destruction bienfaisante et de l'humour, quand tout cela était conjoint en un seul homme, alors c'était moi!

Une fois, dans une critique, vous avez fait allusion à Bergson, conme si, pent-être, les brouillards dans mon

"I believe because, it is absurd!"[39] Tertullian

Recipe for spiritual Life

_____

_____

Raw onions
a spot of garlic
Ginger from Hong Kong
Figs from Smyrna
Dates from Libya
Cold ox blood
Smoked Sturgeon
Black Caviar
Pain Hovis
Horlick's Malted Milk
Grapefruit
Iodine and Milk
Anusol Suppositories
Roast Tenderloin of Pork
Yaourt
Stone Cheese
Jellied Frogs' legs
The back of a heifer
The marrow of a zebra
and a bit o' sassafras!!

cerveau, étarent attribuables à lui mais, mon cher confrère, comme je vous ai expliqué dans *Capricorne*, je n'ai jamais compris cet auteur—sauf par un seul traître mot: *créativité*. Avec ce seul mot enfoncé dans ma tête je l'ai lu conme dans un rêve. Je *sais* qu'il m'a fait du bien, mais je ne sais pas exactement pourquoi. Il n'est pas en outre mon genre de philosophe. Il était pour moi, conme Spengler, aussi un poète à qui je dois les plus hauts enseignements sur le langage. Je n'admets que ce genre de poètes. Tous les autres, dérouté par la musique, me laissent froid. Il n'y a qu'une poésie, à mon avis, et c'est la chanson de signification. La "Voice of Silence", par exemple, répond à tous critères.

Il n'y a pas *deux* attitudes envers le *Verbe* possible. On ne pent pas être prosateur par jour et poète par nuit. Aucune division du travail admissible. Celui qui ne sait pas capturer le tout dans l'ensemble d'une phrase, ou paragraphe, ou livre, ou philosophie même, est foutu. (He falls between the two stools!) Et ceci, alors, est exactement le cas des poètes dépuis Dante! Avec lui "le corps sacré" (Fraenkel) était dispersé. Le *Chant*, par moyen d'un poème, par cette forme-là, devient impossible. La poésie elle-même, ça va sans le dire, n'est jamais perdue. Mais comme la métaphysique se termnait avec Thomas d Aquin, ainsi périssait-t-il ce qu'on appelle par erreur la poésie, avec la mort de Dante. C'est exactement le cas avec la musique. La musique n'est plus possible pour nous. Il y aura une autre musique—bien plus tard—et bien plus céleste, que les démongeaisons d'un Bach, par example. Mais la vraie vie aérienne n'a pas encore commencé. Avec le premier décan du Verseau (Aquarius, en anglais—sic!) il y aura une musique du chaos, c'est à dire une cacophonie de sang et de meurtre. De cette source tragique va renaître le cheval ailé, la chimère que Louis Lambert a (d'après moi, an moins cette chimère), douée d'une vitesse et d'une lumière étourdissante, nous donnera des fornes et pour la poésie, et

"Je suis convaincu que la durée de la vie est en raison de la force que l'individu peut opposer à la pensée; le point d'appui est le Tempérament.... *La vie est un feu qu'il faut couvrir de cendres.* Penser, c'est ajouter de la flamme au feu."[40]

Balzac

———————
———

["I am convinced that the duration of life is due to the force that the individual can oppose to thought; the point of support is the Temperament.... *Life is a fire that must be covered with ashes.* To think is to add flame to fire."]

pour la musique, et pour la métaphysique—une combinaison basée sur le "nombre" et inébranlable—au moins pour 25,960 années. Voilà ce que je prévois et prédis. Et maintenant vous me feriez un grand service si vous ferez une copie de ce petit traité vagabond et le mettrez dans les mains des sacrés gardiens du British Museum pour que la postérité sache bien ce que jai pensé de notre situation dans le temps et l'espace. Ensuite je vous conseille de gargariser la gorge avec deux ou trois lampées de Guinness Stout. Cela vous remettra sur les pieds.

[Translation:

Well, old chap, it will be either you or me—or both! When I read Hermes Trismegistus, I recognized my true master, who was, without a doubt, none other than myself in another incarnation. When I read Lao-tse, it was even more striking! I recognized my own smile where there was magic, beneficent destruction and humor; when all this was combined in one man, why that was me!

Once, in a review, you alluded to Bergson, as if, perhaps, the fog in my brain was attributable to him but, my learned friend, as I explained to you in *Capricorn*, I have never understood this author—except through one traitorous word: creativity. With this one word embedded in my head I read him as in a dream. I know he did me some good, but I don't know exactly why. Besides he is not my kind of philosopher. He was for me like Spengler, also a poet to whom I owe the highest teachings about language. I admit only this kind of poet. All the others, bewildered by music, leave me cold. There is only one poetry, in my opinion, and it is the song of meaning. The "Voice of Silence", for example, meets all criteria.

There are no two attitudes towards the Word possible. One cannot be a be a prose writer by day and a poet by night. No division of labor [is] admissible.

Whoever does not know how to capture the whole in the fullness of a sentence, or paragraph, or book or philosophy itself, is damned. (He falls between the two stools!) And this, then, is exactly the case of the poets since Dante! With him "the sacred body" (Fraenkel) was scattered. Song, by means of a poem, through that very form, becomes impossible. Poetry itself, that goes without saying, is never lost. But as metaphysics ended with Thomas Aquinas, so poetry perished, as it is said, in error, with the death of Dante. It is exactly the case with music. Music is no longer possible for us. There will be another music—much later—and much more heavenly, than the irrepressible desires of a Bach, for example. But real aerial life has not yet begun. With the first decan of Aquarius, (Aquarius in English-sic!) there will be a music of chaos, that is to say a cacophony of blood and murder. From this tragic source will be reborn the winged horse, the chimera that Louis Lambert has (according to me, at least this chimera) endowed with stunning speed and light, which will give us forms for both poetry and music, and for metaphysics—a combination based on "number," and unwavering—at least for 25,960 years. So this is what I foresee and predict. And now you would do me a great favor if you were to make a copy of this little meandering treatise and put it in the hands of the sacred custodians of the British Museum so that posterity will know what I thought of our situation in time and space. Then I advise you to gargle with two or three swigs of Guinness Stout. That will set you back on your feet.]

Nostradamus had the good sense or the tact to forbear prophesying beyond the seven thousandth year. By that time the world, such as we know it, would be engulfed in a great cataclysm—the *fourth* that we know of. But I am looking beyond the cataclysms. I take them in my stride. Whatever we do, *we who survive forever*, has to embrace a vision of the worst and see beyond it.

Bring the vital body and the astral body closer together. Shake well in a solution of passion and extract the desire world. Then mix with aluminum or some other base metal and stick on a spike with a rose in the center. The subliminal rays will create new hormones for the elementals to come. All will be merry and bright in the quincuncial sense.

(Recommended by Paracelse)

My panic at Bordeaux was partly based on a sense of my value for the future. *I could not afford to kick off then*!

When I am ready I will give up the ghost—quite easily and graciously and willingly. *But not a minute before*! I feel that I hold not only my life, but my complete destiny as an imperishable entity in my two hands. I bow to every circumstance, but never surrender the parasol. When I relinquish it, it will not be to do a spectacular high dive (as will happen to Hitler and Mussolini), but to take wing into the blue. I feel that I shall disappear from the earth as mysteriously as Lao-tse and Hermes Trismegistus—or even as Shakespeare, to take a minor case. Tremendous things have happened to me in the short life I have already enjoyed. Greater and more startling things are in store. I feel myself making preparation for them already. I don't need to be told what the Law is, by Edgar and Steiner phlogistons.

I *am* the Law every minute of the day. I am working out the Past, deepening the Present, and paving the Future. All at once. I am lacing myself, like the serpent, about the Caduceus. I am lodging myself in the midst of the constellations as firmly as Draco. And I am leaving a tiny hole at the top for egress, with all due respect to world-destiny. When you rummage through my effects, after my demise, you will see that I have left all sorts of instructions for the men to follow. All the clues can be unraveled, with a little patience. There will not be the slightest mystification for them. All clear as a brook.

Postscriptum

About Fraenkel—
I think the best
thing is to give him
the silence—expunge
him from my con-
sciousness. He was never
properly interred. I will
see to it that he gets
"a fine funeral."

62

And now for the Scherzo! Don't worry about the "Weather Paper!" You can order a copy from C. W. Daniel who is publishing it. Order also from Carrefour, Bruges, a copy of Fraenkel's selected Hamlet Letters! The worms—how can you fight them? You can only crush them, it seems. Kahane I leave to be crushed by the weight of his own inertia. Fraenkel will blow his head off with his own howitzer. When I fire I fire only with trench mortars. When I finally take a good spit I will deluge these bastards. Pax vobiscum! The local color has changed since you last read "Aphrodite!" Read Giono! Read "The Song of the World!" There is a *man* for you—a man of the midi leading his own life in his own unflurried way. And all the world is now listening. No isolated cherub giving out an inaudible warble and dying of exhaustion. The "great poem of death" which Walt Whitman said would one day be written by a "literatus" is now being written. Giono is a sort of Nijinsky who, like St. Francis, managed to preserve that "one invisible indestructible hair." He gives hope, as St. Francis did, by teaching men how to forget. He revives creation. He is writing in words of liquid fire, shot with the gold of the South and of alchemists. He knows the secret of metamorphosis *and* metabolism. He takes the dead midi and buries it in the sunlight. He unwraps the cerements of the forgotten gods and restores them to life. He mythologizes *in the present*. He uses only magical words, words which have been weighed, assayed, tested and purified in his philosophical alembic. If there is hope for France it lies with this man. Everything gets reduced finally to one solitary soul, as Whitman well said. The poet who reaches beyond life kills the dead off! Each bright word, each glinting phrase—and his book is a sheen of magical power—cuts like a sword.

Notice

When short of change for the metro grab a dwarf, saw his hind legs off, wrap carefully in tin foil—or an old newspaper if tin foil is unavailable—and drop them in the box for pneumatiques. You will get an answer in less than 48 hours, C.O.D. When they demand your address just say—Purgatory. It's an ill wind that blows no one some good. A marsh wind, so to speak. All is clover in Honolulu.

He is cutting away the spider webs that enmesh us. He is letting in air and light. He is beating out fine gold in his rhythms. He is killing the cuckoo!

I believe always and only in the lone man, the individual. Giono as a bleeding Colossus stuck in the desert of the South by an accident of Fate. Mark my words—in the next hundred years or so Paris will be extinguished for ever. The real heart of France will be again where it truly belongs— in the midi. It may be that Avignon will supersede Paris. Not Lyons. Not Marseilles. Not Toulouse. Some quiet, unsuspected spot—like Avignon or Arles—I say, will be the seat of the new revitalized France. It must be! Paris is dead—deader even than Louis Lambert's day. Balzac wrote with the scent of death in his nostrils. He was not deceived by the "progress" of the 19th century. He demanded a "superior science" which would reestablish man's relation to God.

Whitman demanded the same thing. The small fry are still wallowing in the prussic acid bath of culture. They are still cradling in the crib of tradition. The past can only be connected with the future by *men*, individuals in whom there is still a soul. Giono has a *soul*—other French writers have taste and learning. They are about as useful to us as the lost Lemurians. And like them, they are born blind. Like them also the modern French writers must be impaled on the spit—in order to "*feel*," in order to develop will-power. Away with the mollusks! The Piscean world of jelly-fish and canned sardines is finished. Give me live sturgeon! Give me the game tuna fish—or if not, *a man*!

The Maginot Line crumbles in its steel and cement casing. No real writer would attempt to defend a frontier which is absurd and needless.

Let Paris perish! Long live Avignon, say I. Live the sun and the faith and the will! Let what is dead rot in the fogs of putrescence.

If your scalp is itchy try Sloan's Liniment. Cut the hairs fine and bend gently with a sharp tweezer. If they fall out circularly you are of Aryan stock and can vote in the next election. The Lemurians were covered with hair. It prevented them from being singed during the volcanic eruptions. They were happy in their way, tho' not possessed of memory.

Recipe for Artist:

Mornings a cold douche and a brisk walk around the block seven times. Breakfast in bed with the telephone handy. A little cod-liver oil with the coffee gives a color to the cheeks. Write slowly and without passion. The first thoughts are the best. Think back to the next to the last reincarnation and imagine what you would have said then had you known you would be what you are now. Look forward to the next day if possible. Keep sanguine and pay all bills promptly.

Leave England to her empire and France to her colonies. The true precincts of France and England are differently circumscribed. When I touch a man like Giono I touch the real France.

Everything hangs now by a slender thread. Either we are going to preserve "the silver cord" which connects with the heart, or we are going to sever it. Never was there such a momentous decision to be made.

Donc Scherzo! Allez-oop! The sirens are blowing again—or was it yesterday? Black Thursday. The war panic. The worm's idle fear. The patriot's lust for defense. The harlot's joy. The editors' anguish. But the poet shrieks with joy! The poet loves to hear the sound of approaching disaster. Calamity is his iodine. Let the warriors eat their victory. Victory is the iodoform of the splintered soul. The great poem of death is in the life which surrounds us—the chemical hallucinations, the Bigorrian fervor, the apostatic ecstasy of Paris-Soir, the marble of the unveined masterpieces which clutter the counting houses. Shriek sirens, and blow down the noxious gases! Open wide the lethal chambers. Kill with teeth and nails and tuning forks! Spread the barrage, rattle the rusty sabres. "Time is ample" Ah Yes! Catalepsy is only inverted ecstasy. Enthusiasm in its lesser manifestations is madness. Belief is criminal when it is only supported by frogs and idiots. Blow down the cathedrals! Extinguish the libraries. Crumble museums and morgues and printing presses! Take all the apparati away. Leave me a hunk of coal, a sharp stone, a bit of yellow ochre or Irish green.

Scherzo! Tremble ye flute strings! Tremble and twitch! Fuck your black Thursdays and your screeching sirens! Fuck your Dolomites and stalagmites, your trained cobras and your lack-luster toads. The music has begun. The earth yawns. God is rolling over in his sleep, drugged with love, bored with beneficence.

When friends come who bore the shit out of you—sit tight on the edge of the chair and count the minutes as they tick off. Listen attentively and think what you would say yourself if you had their intelligence. Compare accounts, subtract for scientific inaccuracies, smile now and then or yawn carelessly while keeping up a rapid fire exchange of gim-crack jokes and other odds and ends. Keep a hatchet near the door and as you say Good Night swing it lustily!

To stimulate the appetite, carnal or spiritual, try "Sidereal Salts"— a medieval remedy. The garnered sweat of toads is also recommended. More for the sexual appetite, however.
HVM

Poets, do nothing! Absolutely nothing. Everything is *grand* just as it is. Cease firing your fire-crackers. Stop scratching with the pen. Close the typewriter. Your place is in the bomb shelter. Hide below with the other rats. Bring a moist rag to stuff in your mouth. Hold your breath until you can count 91, 476, 392 1/2! Be Yogi! Be Beelzebubs! Be Luciferian! The devil is abroad and the air is foul with pestilence.

Scherzo! Wilder the strings! Steadier, men, steadier—or the fiddles will snap! Have you a bit of resin handy? Have you a drop of arnica? And where is our old friend Halitosis? Where the friendly mansard that will house a same idea? Show me not the ruins, show me not the caves. Unfurl your logarithms now—we need you, O valiant X and Y and minus 4.

This time no hero will sing you to sleep. This time no salt is available for sowing the dead fields with death. Everything and everybody has been packed off to the chemical works. Nothing functions but the siren. Nothing bleeds, not even the left ventricle of the heart.

We are all lost in the Mammoth Cave of Fear. We are with the stalactites and the stalagmites. We are with the organ's echo and the fife's mad whistle. In the bowels of the earth we are safe—until the roof caves in and crushes us. Vivent les cavemans, les cavernes les grottes, et *les crottes*! [Long live the cavemen, the caverns, the grottos and *the turds*!] Cruds we are and cruds we remain. A horse's wet fart—and out tumble a few bright cruds. A siren's shrill blast and bango! we are poisoned to the marrow. Stiffen not, ye spineless wretches. Fall limp in you own sweet shit. Gather the wind, stuff your ears, shell your peanuts. Time marches on. The wheel turns. The grape is pressed. The juice flows. The victory turns rancid.

If you can't sleep—try to keep awake forever. Hold one eye open with a dropper and let the other eye close firmly. Remind yourself constantly that you are awake. Do all the things you intended to do during the day. Don't fall asleep! Think of some adept of the White Brotherhood Lodge in Zulu Land. Think of how he is thinking about you, looking after you. He never sleeps—why should you! When the alarm goes off get up and go back to sleep.

THE WEATHER PAPER

"Fair and warmer, with light easterly clouds of poison gas."

Do I smell something?

Is it the toast burning?

No? Oh—flesh burning—that's it? Good, save me a slice for next Wednesday when I shall be famished. Have you a drop of Ketchup per chance? *Blue Label*, preferably. If not, a bit o' cow dung!

From a letter to Richard Osborn—

"*To my Grandmother* I enjoyed. I know it appeared in Delta—error on my part, saying Booster. *Doodletown* I considered a superior thing, and in the true American tradition, *better for what it is than many of the things Robinson or Frost have done.* That's my opinion. Cooney has his and we don't always meet....."

Signed—Michael Fraenkel

NOTE: I will use this as a blurb when I publish Osborn's poems.

And now rallentando... A tree to sit under, a book to read, a mineral to study for the hidden dwarfs. The influences! Why yes, and the confluences too. Subtract all the planetary rays from the metals, gather the moon dust and the Uranium and all the chromospheres and photospheres as yet undenominated—still we shall have only *mystery*. While the researchers research the cosmos creates new problems. The Theosophists want to "know" God's ways; the Occultists want to reveal what is hidden; but the Sage leaves everything in its place and in its aura. The mystery is at the center, and no matter how many dimensions we evolve we don't shake the mystery out of the bag. Edgar walks the streets of London working out axioms. Fred pulps the sensitive neurones to unlatch a fleeting emotion. Reichel locks himself in his room to paint Loneliness. Moricand varnishes the Pompeiian phallus to rub his hands over an antique symbol. Fraenkel lies on his silken couch and dreams of death, but being dead mistakes the dream for death. Nobody pierces the vacuum, nobody gets inside the barometer. The planets slip and roll like gobs of mercury. The suns unglue from the starry firmament. Night falls regularly and with it the nightmare.

All is unwritten law—undecipherable law. Hammurabi, Zoroaster, Moses, Akhenaton, Solon, Solomon, Hermes, Nebuchadnezzar—even the grocer—all have their *Law*. While we figure it out one way, the Australian Bushmen are decoding some other cipher. Everybody is equipped with their own right antennae. That noise of scrambled electricity you get on the radio—what's that, pray? Are the laws intermingling? Is it Rudolph trying to get a word in edgeways from the other sphere?

For the poet the crackle of static is sublime music. The "interferences" are better than the concerts or the publicity talks.

The Soundless Sound
or
The Voice of Nada

?

To thoroughly enjoy what you have just written—wrap it up and send it from one planet to another. Get the opinions of all the root race men—and the opinions of their wives if possible. Start translating your work in unknown tongues. Use the conative subjunctives—and the ablative once in a while. Don't explain your work to any one. Just pass it round like you would the hat. Remember that there are angels who still wear hats. But even Swedenborg forgot the condom!

"Les prophètes et les voyants sont le plus souvent des êtres qui apparemment sont plongés dans une stupidité végétative; ils ne gaspillent pas leurs énergies psychiques; elles dorment en eux dans une abondance pleine et latente."41

Balzac

[Prophets and seers are most often beings who apparently are immersed in a vegetative stupidity; they do not waste their psychic energies; they sleep in them in full and latent abundance."]

When you hear the gong strike it will be exactly a quarter to twelve. The corpse speaking from above Greenwich somewhere Hallucinating. *She* is gone, but the *Voice* still gives the correct time. But who asked for the correct time? Who asked that this Voice be preserved from the grave?

We are now in the Ides of March, according to the Julian calendar. But what say the Toltecs? What time is it in Amerindia? The walruses are basking in the Antarctic sun. They know no time, no axioms, no God, no problems. We have "dominion" over them, as they say. Good! But have we any sunshine, any ice-cakes to float on? Tomorrow it will be Louis Lambert again, a new link in the endless chain of words which when all melded together will make sense. But I'd rather be a walrus. From Balzac to God is a long and difficult journey. No half-way stations that I can see. No ale and porter, no kidney pies. Degenerate and you become the walrus. Defunct in soul, but alive chemically, toxically, marsupially. Apparently. God is not much interested in retrograde matter. He likes the organon. He wants us all to be individuals so that when we melt into the Super-Self we will make a strong soup. I say, kill the black doves of death and let's have mock turtle soup. The old serpent power will outlast the dynamo. "Draco and the Ecliptic"—I am beginning to smell my theme—the good old Kundalini theme. Picasso began to really paint like a genius when he lost his "feeling." He can do almost anything with the brush, but he can't kill the black doves. Joyce pried open the lid of Pandora's box and saw the snakes coiled one within the other. In the middle of all creation is a river which seems like pure gold but if you wade into it you turn to stone. If you follow the wheel of life you have no need to ford the river. The Chinese knew that when they invented the river that runs through the middle of their chess board. Whoever crossed that river never returned, except *"as an enemy"*—italics mine. To put the King in the middle of the board, in the exact center, was to give mate. Why? Because not even the King is permitted to penetrate the mystery.

Do you sometimes hear voices? They are the root souls speaking. Some get lost in the shuffle and can't find an unrented body. The real devils, according to an authentic source, are the Zwinglis who are constantly shelling peanuts whilst searching for the Absolute. Though they use only the etheric body the shells are so dry and brittle that the tread of etheric feet makes a noise like lice cracking under the hammer.

It was putting him in the water-closet they said. Aye, and there he might sit and ponder for eternity. Caught in the hub of the wheel, the prisoner of knowledge, seeing all, knowing all, and yet absolutely powerless. Desire is what makes the wheel go round. The hub is nothing without the desire to make it revolve. When the termites get up to go on a rampage it is always in the night and always they choose the most obscure route through the forest. They move without eyes, in the dark, amidst the most bewildering obstacles. Nothing can stop them. Their armor is impenetrable, their wisdom infallible. Be a termite, brother, if you would attain your goal. Set out from the blackest depths of the forest on the darkest night with the blindest eyes. To be truly occult does not mean to seek light—it means to seek the source and the source is everywhere at once—if you have the least speck or crumb of desire. When the Light of Asia began to enlighten the world he ceased drinking from the source. The moment he turned his face to the world he lost his power.

Enlightenment is a form of intoxication like any other. More subtle and poisonous perhaps, because seemingly unselfish. But the truly unselfish thing is egotism. The veil is rent only when one attempts to be more or less than he is. The man who is only himself violates nothing. The man who follows his desires really desires nothing. He demonstrates the validity of desire—that's all.

And now, O son of Jupiter, the greatest affliction is to be beneficent without being yourself. Jupiterian souls are beneficent and prodigal because they cannot help being so. They are old gods in degenerate form. They help the universe along because they belong to the universe. They do not reckon in "parts," but only in "wholes." They have stupendous success so long as they are blind and trusting, confident that Providence is with them. The moment they intervene as "knowing," cunning agents, they are lost. Good fortune is not the result of wisdom so much as of a royal nature. The wise man develops into a prudent man.

"Bestride the Bird
of Life if thou wouldst
know."
From the "Book of the Golden
Precepts."

_____

The prudent man wastes time calculating possibilities and probabilities. He relies only on wisdom. But the greatest wisdom is born of blindness—born of the heart's impulse. The heart is an organ which cannot be cultivated like a hothouse flower. It is developed only under duress, in moments of utter recklessness. The "occult" lads *talk* about the heart, but look to the kidney and spleen. They would do away with sorrow and evil, but sorrow and evil are nourishment for the heart. And when the heart is full-grown, it will dispense with sorrow and evil as the soil dispenses with the fertilizer when it has had its fill. The heart *converts* everything to cosmic uses. Wisdom converts nothing—it is merely the gleam of the electric light which can be switched on or off, according to the commutator's functioning. The first word to be said for the cosmos is that it is "magnificent!" All the other words come later, and are poorer. Beside splendor and magnificence "truth" stinks like a dead vulture.

Son of Jupiter, I counsel you to forget about the Path. *Be* the path as you blaze your way, but don't *try* to be anything. Be only what you desire to be. There you must be undivided. The devil will always be lying across the path. The devil is your best friend, if you accept him for what he is. Wear no amulets, carry no charms. Invite the "elementals" to dwell with you as you would your best friend.

Do nothing for profit's sake, or for appearances, or for fame or glory. Never compromise, even with God. Better a flat defeat than a half-assed victory. Better a thousand defeats than a victory which is not rightfully your own. Better Beelzebub than Lucifer if Beelzebub is your heart's desire.

Keep the wheel turning and the light will come of its own accord. Don't be an Occultist—*be occult*!

Henry
3/14/39

79

Footnotes:

1. (IZB): *An Introduction to Zen Buddhism* by Daisetz Teitaro Suzuki, Grove Press, Black Cat Edition 1964, 43.

2. IZB, 43, Victor Hugo quoted from Richard of Saint Victor.

3. IZB, 55.

4. IZB, 68.

5. IZB, 68, inspired by Shuzan.

6. IZB, 68.

7. IZB, 71.

8. IZB, 74.

9. After explaining the mystery of Osiris, Éliphas Lévi interprets the riddle posed to Oedipus to mean: "Divine or die."
(HoM): The History of Magic by Éliphas Lévi, 506:
"Divine or die—such was the terrible dilemma proposed by the sphinx to the Candidates for Theban royalty. The reason is that the secrets of science are actually those of life; the alternatives are to reign or to serve, to be or not to be. The natural forces will break us if we do not put them to use for the conquest of the world. There is no mean between the height of kinghood and the abyss of the victim state, unless we are content to be counted among those who are nothing because they ask not why or what they are."

10. IZB, 74, answer from Joshu (Chao-chou) when asked what the Tao or the truth of Zen is.

11. IZB, 74.

12. IZB, 75, dialog between Sekito and his disciple Yakusan (Yueh-shan).

13. IZB, 80, answer by Daiju on what is the Mind if there is no Mind independent of words.

14. IZB, 86, expression in the Prajnaparamita Sutras.

15. IZB, 92, in section on satori.

16. IZB, 94, from Tokusan (Te-shan) when he gained an insight into the truth of Zen and he burned his manuscripts of Diamond Sutra that he had valued so much that he carried them everywhere.

17. IZB, 95.

18. IZB, 95.

19. IZB, 96.

20. HoM, 516.

21. (RCC): *The Rosicrucian Cosmo-Conception, or, Mystic Christianity: An Elementary Treatise Upon Man's Past Evolution, Present Constitution and Future Development*, by Max Heindel, 77.

22. RCC, 286, in section Rosicrucian Cosmo-Conception. In Miller's copy at UCLA, he double underlined "note" in the margin.

23. HoM, 521.

24. HoM, 524.

25. HoM, 527.

26. HoM, 527.

27. RCC, 293, in section Evolution on the Earth. In Miller's copy he wrote "Veil of Isis, Holy of Holies" at the top of the page. He underlined a note next to this phrase and put arrows in the inner and outer margins pointing to it with "HM vs *June!*"

28. RCC, 273, in section Influence of Mercury. In Miller's copy he wrote two vertical lines next to the phrase.

29. HoM, 505.

30. HoM, 510.

31. RCC, 277, in section Rosicrucian Cosmo-Conception.

32. RCC, 283, in section Evolution on the Earth. In Miller's copy he wrote two vertical lines next to the phrase.

33. RCC, 286, in section The Lucifer Spirits. In Miller's copy he wrote "Quille phrase!"

34. HoM, 13.

35. HoM, 18.

36. HoM, 19.

37. HoM, 35.

38. Miller and Moricand thought that Virgil had predicted the age of Pisces and Miller thought Balzac predicted the age of Aquarius. Moricand's article was a response to: *Il y a toujours eu des directeurs de conscience en Occident* that appeared in Volontés Numéro Spécial, 1939. That response is on pages 219–222, of the next issue (probably number 19 in July of 1939). It talks about the upcoming age of Aquarius.

..... "If Virgil returned among us, he could sing of the new advent as he sang of the approaching one 2,000 years ago. The situation is the same. Next to the astrologers, new Magi who announce its arrival, who will be the inspired poet who will celebrate the advent of Ganymede, symbol of Aquarius and of the initiate who was carried up to the sky of Knowledge by the eagle of Jupiter?"

39. The consensus of Tertullian scholars is that the reading "I believe because it is absurd" sharply diverges from Tertullian's own thoughts, given the priority placed on reasoned argument and rationality in his writings. In the same work, Tertullian later writes "But here again, I must have some reasons."Elsewhere, he writes that the new Christian "should believe nothing but that nothing should be rashly believed."

Scholars note further examples of where Tertullian acts by following a method of reasoned argument. The meaning of the phrase may relate to 1 Corinthians 1:17–31, where something foolish to a human may be a part of God's wisdom, or Tertullian may be repeating an idea rehearsed in Aristotle's Rhetoric, where Aristotle argues that something is more credibly true if it is an incredible claim, on the reason that it would not have been made up if it were truly so incredible to the human mind. Eric Osborn concludes that "the classic formula credo quia absurdum (even when corrected to quia ineptum) does not represent the thought of Tertullian." [from Wikipedia]

40. From *Les Martyrs Ignorés* by Balzac.
41. From *Balzac* by Ernst Robert Curtius, 82.

More information about Miller's other handwritten books is at:
henrymillersuniquebooks.com

Index

Acknowledgments

I thank my family, Adrienne, Porsha, Mike and Quinn for understanding that when I am in the cave of archiving, transcribing, editing, illustrating, formatting and connecting that I do this work in a focused and intense manner.

I thank the Miller scholars who have helped me or inspired me: Roger Jackson, Michael Paduano, James Decker, Arthur Hoyle, Magnus Toren and Karl Orend.

I thank Paula McNally who was indispensable as a remote researcher.

I am grateful to Erika Grundmann who reached out to me about spelling on my web page. In reading her web page about her George Dibbern book, I discovered her expertise in French translation. With hope, I asked for help and she graciously came through.

www.ingramcontent.com/pod-product-compliance
Lightning Source LLC
Chambersburg PA
CBHW051234090426
42740CB00001B/12